My
HOSPITAL
PRAYER
and Activities
BOOK

This book is dedicated to my parents, David and Eileen.

Fr Peter-Michael Scott

Illustrations by Jane Morgan

redemptorist
publications

NOTES FOR KIDS

Always ask an adult to help you cut out.

Have a shoebox-sized container with a lid to keep your treasures in. Keep cards and pictures from school friends and relatives inside – things you want to save. Label and decorate it with pictures or stickers.

ACTIVITY

JESUS IS ALWAYS WITH YOU! Can you find me on every spread?

NOTES FOR ADULTS

USEFUL THINGS TO HAVE FOR THE ACTIVITIES

Blank cards with envelopes, thin card, washable felt-tips, wax crayons, coloured pencils, scrapbook for letters, stickers, washable glue stick, sticky tape, spiral-bound notebook, little box containing a variety of coloured cards on which to write and scissors for cutting.

Difficulty levels:

EASY MEDIUM HARD

Published by **Redemptorist Publications**

Alphonsus House, Chawton, Hampshire, GU34 3HQ, UK
Tel: +44 (0)1420 88222, Fax: +44 (0)1420 88805
Email: rp@rpbooks.co.uk
www.rpbooks.co.uk
A registered charity limited by guarantee
Registered in England 3261721

First published September 2013

Editors: Yvonne Fordyce and Lisa Gregoire
Design: Jeni Carew
Illustrations: Jane Morgan

ISBN 978-0-85231-405-0

A CIP catalogue record for this book is available from the British Library.

Concordat cum originali: Ann Blackett.

Imprimatur: + Kieran Conry, Bishop of Arundel and Brighton, 23 August 2013.

The publisher acknowledges help from the parish of St John Fisher, Shepperton, Helena Duckett and Beverley Purcell.

The publisher gratefully acknowledges permission to use the following copyright material in this book:

Excerpts from the English translation and chants of *The Roman Missal* © 2010, International Commission on English in the Liturgy Corporation. All rights reserved.

Excerpts from *The Jerusalem Bible*, copyright © 1966 by Darton, Longman & Todd, Ltd and Doubleday, a division of Random House, Inc. Reprinted by permission.

Excerpts from the *Good News Bible* © 1994, 2004 published by the Bible Societies/Harper Collins Publishers Ltd UK, *Good News Bible* © American Bible Society 1966, 1971, 1976, 1992. Used with permission.

Rites on pp 30–39 from *Pastoral Care of the Sick,* copyright © 1983 by Catholic Book Publishing Corp., New Jersey.

Printed by Advent Colour, Andover, SP10 3LU.

CONTENTS

INTRODUCTION 6

TALKING TO GOD 8
- Talking to God and some prayers to get you started

SAINTS' STORIES 16
- St Camillus and St Bernadette
- A fingerprint Rosary
- Praying the Joyful Mysteries

BIBLE STORIES 24
- Imagine...
- A paper boat and a life jacket

BLESSING AND SACRAMENTS 30
- Receiving the sacraments
- Reconciliation: time to say sorry
- Holy Communion: meeting Jesus
- Anointing of the sick: giving strength

PRAYERS TO PICK AND CHOOSE 40

RESOURCES BACK COVER

5

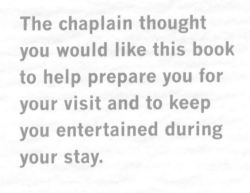

HELLO!

teacher

The chaplain thought you would like this book to help prepare you for your visit and to keep you entertained during your stay.

Each page is packed with fun activities and stories, which will help you to grow closer to Jesus. This book will also help you to say your prayers, learn about the sacraments, meet some of the saints and biblical characters, and discover interesting new things about your Catholic faith.

COLOUR US IN

surgeon

paramedic

For some of the activities, you will need some help - that's where your family and friends come in. The hospital chaplain will also be on hand to help too.

receptionist

HARD ACTIVITY

During your stay, you will also meet other people who work in the hospital. They are there to care for you. Can you work out who's who in the pictures below?

granny

nurse

TALKING TO GOD...

and some prayers to get you started.

Hospital is very different from being at home, so it is quite normal that it will feel a little strange. Say the prayers that you are used to saying and let God take away your worries.

TALK TO GOD

To begin: make the
sign of the cross and say,
**In the name of the Father,
and of the Son,
 and of the Holy Spirit. Amen.**

You may know this next prayer
that Jesus taught us. We say it
together at Mass. You may also say
the **Our Father** at home with your
family, or with your class at school.

EASY
ACTIVITY

Decorate
and colour
the frame
around the
prayer.

Our Father, who art in heaven,
hallowed be thy name;
thy kingdom come,
thy will be done
on earth as it is in heaven.
Give us this day our daily bread,
and forgive us our trespasses,
as we forgive those who trespass against us;
and lead us not into temptation,
but deliver us from evil.
Amen.

If you are feeling ill, you can say this prayer:
Lord Jesus, I feel ill.
Help me to be brave
and kind to the people looking after me.
Thank you for being here with me.
Amen.

COLOUR ME IN

Say this prayer when you're feeling a little better:
Thank you, Jesus, for helping me. Also, thank you for those who are looking after me. Amen.

COLOUR ME IN

A closing prayer:
Glory be to the Father,
and to the Son,
and to the Holy Spirit,
as it was in the beginning,
is now, and ever shall be,
world without end.
Amen.

Our Lady is very good at praying for us, especially when we forget, or when we are asleep.

When we say the Hail Mary prayer, we ask Mary, the mother of Jesus, to pray for us.

Hail, Mary, full of grace,
the Lord is with thee.
Blessed art thou among women,
and blessed is the fruit of thy womb,
    Jesus.
Holy Mary, Mother of God,
pray for us sinners,
now and at the hour of our death.
Amen.

HOSPITAL ENTRANCE

MEDIUM ACTIVITY

Help Granny to find her grandson in hospital.

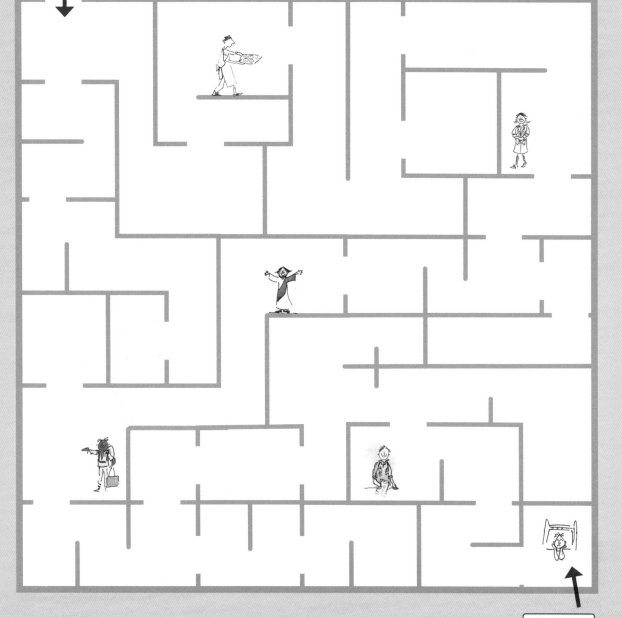

GRANDSON

Take a look around the hospital ward and see who else you can pray for:

Perhaps somebody new has arrived.

> Dear Jesus,
> please take care of all of us on this ward, especially (name) ....
> who has just arrived.
> Amen.

Fill in the gaps in the prayer.

COLOUR ME IN

A prayer for my family:

> God, our Father, please look after my family while I am in hospital, especially (names) ....
> ....
> ....
> and ....
> Keep them close to you while they are looking after me.
> Help me to show them how much I love them.
> Amen.

COLOUR ME IN

Fill in the gaps in the prayer.

It's impossible to get to sleep!

Try saying the following prayer very slowly until you feel drowsy:
Be with me, Lord, I love you above all things.

A prayer for the doctors and nurses who are looking after me:

A prayer for all children and young people in hospital:

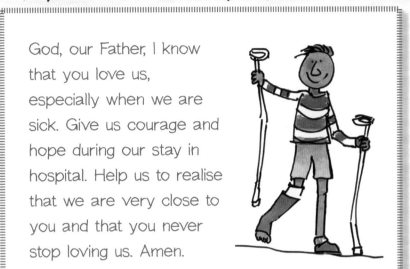

God, our Father, I know that you love us, especially when we are sick. Give us courage and hope during our stay in hospital. Help us to realise that we are very close to you and that you never stop loving us. Amen.

God, our Father, help the doctors and nurses who are taking care of me. Give them gentle hands; give them understanding and patience. They are doing your work when they look after me. Amen.

I must always remember to eat and drink what the nurse or doctor recommends.

COLOUR ME IN

A prayer before meals:
God, our Father, we thank you for our food and drink. Bless us and all those who are staying in this hospital. Also, bless those who are poor, homeless and hungry. Amen.

13

A CLOSING PRAYER

 You may want to end your prayers with the sign of the cross, just as we began:
In the name of the Father, and of the Son, and of the Holy Spirit. Amen.

You can talk to God in any way you want, and you can make up your own prayers — speaking from your heart. If you need help, ask someone else to write the prayer for you. Here are some ideas on what to say:

Dear Jesus,
I have something special to ask you:
....
....
....
....
Thank you for always being with me.
Amen.

Dear Jesus, I want to say a special prayer to you:
....
....

Thank you, Jesus,
for listening to me.
Amen.

Dear Jesus, today I felt
....
....
God bless ....
and ....
and ....
Amen.

Dear Jesus, thank you for today. It was fun when we
....
....
God bless all my friends.
....
Amen.

EASY ACTIVITY

FIND A FRIEND

Look out for a new child on your ward. What can you do to be friendly, to show that you know they are there and that you want to talk to them? Smile? Draw a picture or write a note saying who you are and ask someone to take it to the child?

MEDIUM ACTIVITY

Draw around your hand. In each finger write or draw your own prayer.

SAINTS' STORIES

THE STORY OF ST CAMILLUS

St Camillus de Lellis is the patron saint of the sick, hospitals, nurses and doctors.

Camillus was born on 25 May 1550 in Italy. He always wanted to be a soldier, like his father, so he joined the army as soon as he could. He fought in many battles. But he also led a wild and irresponsible life for many years, getting into quarrels, fighting and living just for himself, with little regard for anyone else.

He suffered an injury to his leg while still a young man. This affected him for forty-six years. Camillus tried many times to change his way of life, but returned again and again to his old, bad ways.

Then one day Camillus found his way into a church. There he met a priest who talked about Jesus' love for each of us. This inspired Camillus.

He knew there and then that he wanted to dedicate his life to God, and to help nurse and care for people who were ill and had to spend time in hospital.

As an ordained priest, Camillus formed what would eventually become the Order of St Camillus. His followers travelled throughout Europe, providing care to those who were sick, injured or dying. People recognised Camillus and his followers because they always wore a red cross on their black garments.

Camillus always suffered pain in his leg during the remainder of his life, but he went on to establish hospitals all over Italy. The injury to his leg was a constant reminder to treat those who are ill with kindness and patience.

He died aged sixty-four, doing what he loved: caring for those who are sick.

If you want St Camillus to pray for you and others, say:

St Camillus, pray for us.

SAINTS' NAMES

Are you named after a saint? Do you know their life story? Did you know that you can ask any saint to pray for you? Simply say, St (name), pray for us. **We read about the lives of saints and sometimes feel close enough to pray to them for help and guidance.**

What do you think St Camillus looked like? Try making a stand-up model of Camillus.

1 Fold a rectangle of thick paper in half. Using the template below, draw half of the outline of Camillus against the fold.

2 Cut around the shape, unfold the paper and lay it flat.

Template

Always ask an adult to help you cut out.

COLOUR ME IN

MEDIUM ACTIVITY

See if you can answer these questions about St Camillus:

What did St Camillus injure?
A) **ARM**
B) **LEG**
C) **NOSE**

What colour cross did his followers wear?
A) **GREEN**
B) **YELLOW**
C) **RED**

What do you say if you want St Camillus to pray for you and others?

ANSWERS: B; C; St Camillus, pray for us.

18

3 Using felt-tip pens draw and colour his eyes, nose and ears. Remember to add his red cross.

4 Now stand him up and say, **St Camillus, pray for us.**

COLOUR ME IN

EASY ACTIVITY

Which one of these nurses is the odd one out?

A B C D

ANSWER: C.

THE STORY OF ST BERNADETTE

St Bernadette is the patron saint of the sick.

Marie-Bernarde Soubirous was born in Lourdes, France, on 7 January 1844. As a child she was called Bernadette. Her family was very poor and lived in a one-room basement, called the dungeon. She was not a very strong child and suffered from colds and asthma.

On 11 February 1858, Bernadette, then aged fourteen, was out gathering firewood with her sister Marie and a friend near the grotto of Massabielle.

While the other girls crossed the little stream in front of the grotto and walked on, Bernadette stayed behind, looking for a place to cross where she wouldn't get her stockings wet. She sat outside the grotto and started to take off her stockings when she heard the sound of rushing wind. From the dark alcove "came a dazzling light and a white figure". This was the first of eighteen visions of what Bernadette would later call "a small young lady".

When Bernadette told her family about the vision, they did not believe her, but the Blessed Virgin Mary, "Our Lady", kept reappearing.

One day, Our Lady told Bernadette to dig where she stood, and a fresh spring of water came bubbling out of the ground. The people who were blind and who washed their faces in the spring could see. Those who were sick and who washed their bodies in the water became well.

Our Lady told Bernadette to build a great church there. This came to be known as the Shrine of Lourdes. Many miracles still happen there to this day.

During her early life in Lourdes and when she later became a nun, Bernadette never forgot to say the Rosary.

If you want St Bernadette to pray for you and others, say:

St Bernadette, pray for us.

20

EASY

ACTIVITY

Colour in St Bernadette.

A

B

EASY ACTIVITY

Can you spot five differences between the two Marys (above)?

ST BERNADETTE AND THE ROSARY

The Rosary is a special prayer that has been said for many years on beads like those on the right. It tells the story of Jesus and his mother, Mary.

When we pray the Rosary, we say simple prayers, like the **Our Father** and **Hail Mary**.

The Rosary prayer begins with the sign of the cross (at the crucifix), followed by one Our Father, three Hail Marys and one Glory be to the Father.

The Rosary has five groups of ten beads. Each group is called a decade, which means "ten". We say one Our Father, ten Hail Marys and one Glory be to the Father. While we say these prayers, we think of stories about Jesus. We call these stories "mysteries".

There are five Joyful Mysteries; five Luminous Mysteries; five Sorrowful Mysteries and five Glorious Mysteries. These mysteries cover the whole of the life of Jesus and the life of his mother, Mary.

If you get tired, don't worry! When St Bernadette was a child she could only manage to say one decade of the Rosary (one Our Father, ten Hail Marys and one Glory be to the Father) before she had to give up.

ANSWERS: Mary's veil; Mary's eyes; Mary's collar; Jesus' top; Jesus' leg.

MEDIUM ACTIVITY

1) Mark your little finger with a waterproof felt-tip pen.

2) Print it on the circles of the Rosary.

TRY SAYING
THE ROSARY.
Begin with the Joyful
Mysteries. These are happy stories.
The other mysteries can come later.

The First Joyful Mystery is the Annunciation.
The angel Gabriel tells Mary that she is
going to be the mother of Jesus. When
we find things difficult to do, let us trust
in God to help us.

**The Second Joyful Mystery is the
Visitation**. Mary visits her cousin Elizabeth
to tell her how happy she is that Elizabeth is
going to have a baby. When someone needs
some love and care, let us be the one to
offer help.

**The Third Joyful
Mystery is the
Nativity**. Jesus is born in
Bethlehem. Help us to share what
we have with those who are poor.

**The Fourth Joyful Mystery is the
Presentation**. Mary and Joseph
bring baby Jesus to the Temple to
present him to the Lord. Let us
pray that we follow the guidance
of our parents.

**The Fifth Joyful Mystery is the
Finding of Jesus in the Temple**.
Mary and Joseph find Jesus in
the Temple, where he is talking to
people about God. Teach me,
Lord Jesus, to stay close to you.

BIBLE STORIES

Listen to, or read, this story from the Bible.
Then try the imagination challenge that follows it.

JESUS THE HEALER

Chaplain/
priest:

A reading from the holy Gospel according to Mark.

Child,
visitor:

Glory to you, O Lord.

Mark 10:46-52

As Jesus left Jericho with his disciples and a large crowd, Bartimaeus, a blind beggar, was sitting at the side of the road. When he heard that it was Jesus of Nazareth, he began to shout and to say, "Son of David, Jesus, have pity on me."

And many of them scolded him and told him to keep quiet, but he only shouted all the louder, "Son of David, have pity on me." Jesus stopped and said, "Call him here." So they called the blind man. "Courage," they said, "get up; he is calling you." So throwing off his cloak, he jumped up and went to Jesus. Then Jesus spoke, "What do you want me to do for you?"

"Rabbuni," the blind man said to him, "Master, let me see again." Jesus said to him, "Go; your faith has saved you." And immediately his sight returned and he followed him along the road.

Chaplain/
priest:

The Gospel of the Lord.

Child,
visitor:

Praise to you, Lord Jesus Christ.

COLOUR
ME IN

IMAGINE

As your visitor slowly reads the words below, close your eyes and picture the scene:

**Jesus is walking onto your hospital ward.
There is a large group of people around
him. He cannot see you, so you shout out
"Jesus, Master, over here!"
He stops, looks around and asks,
"Who called me?"
"Jesus, Master, come over here," you shout.
He looks in your direction, and is soon
standing next to you.
Jesus says, "What do you want me to do for you?"
Calmly tell Jesus how you want him to help you.
Hear him say to you, "Go; your faith has saved you."**

A thank you to Jesus:

Dear Jesus, that story
made me feel

....

....

EASY (ACTIVITY)

Draw doctors, nurses and children who are on your ward.

JESUS CALMS A STORM

Chaplain/ priest: **A reading from the holy Gospel according to Mark.**

Child, visitor: Glory to you, O Lord.

Mark 4:35-41

With the coming of evening, Jesus said to his disciples, "Let us cross over to the other side." And leaving the crowd behind they took him, just as he was, in the boat; and there were other boats with him. Then it began to blow a gale and the waves were breaking into the boat so that it was almost swamped. But he was in the stern, his head on the cushion, asleep. They woke him and said to him, "Master, do you not care? We are going down!" And he woke up and rebuked the wind and said to the sea, "Quiet now! Be calm!" And the wind dropped, and all was calm again. Then he said to them, "Why are you so frightened? How is it that you have no faith?" They were filled with awe and said to one another, "Who can this be? Even the wind and the sea obey him."

COLOUR ME IN

Chaplain/ priest: **The Gospel of the Lord.**

Child, visitor: Praise to you, Lord Jesus Christ.

IMAGINE

Imagine you are in a boat with the disciples and Jesus. What sort of boat is it? Can you smell the sea? Can you feel the waves rocking the boat? Jesus is asleep.

It starts to rain. The sky has dark clouds. Jesus is still asleep. The wind picks up and blows hard against the boat. The waves begin to get very high. Jesus is still asleep. A thunderclap and lightning dart across the sky. Jesus is still asleep.

Now imagine waking Jesus from his sleep. He yawns, stretches his arms, stands up and looks at you. Hear him say to you, "Quiet now, be calm. Why are you so frightened?"

Tell Jesus what frightens you. It might not be the storm; it might be something about your stay in hospital.

Imagine Jesus calming the storm. The wind drops, the rain stops and the sun starts to brighten the sky.

A thank you to Jesus:

> Dear Jesus, that story made me feel
> ....
> ....

EASY ACTIVITY

Write about or draw your boat here...

HOW TO MAKE THE DISCIPLES' BOAT

Have some stiff paper ready for the boat. When a friend, a brother or sister, or mum or dad comes to see you, let them help you to make the boat.

One of you could read out the instructions, or you could each have a go at making a boat.

1 Start with a rectangular piece of paper, long side up. Fold in half, then open.

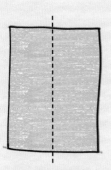

2 Fold in half downwards; crease well.

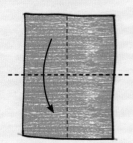

3 Fold corners down to meet the centre line. Crease the folds well.

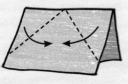

4 Fold uppermost layer upwards and do the same to the back. Crease well.

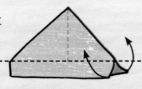

5 Pull the sides out and then flatten.

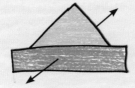

6 Fold front layer up to the top. Do the same to the back.

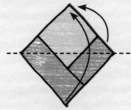

7 Pull sides outwards and flatten.

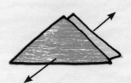

8 Gently pull the top parts of the model outwards, making a boat shape.

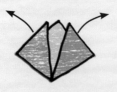

9 Flatten well to crease all folds. Then open out slightly, forming a boat!

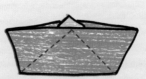

Trust in Jesus

Dear Jesus, when I am afraid help me to remember that you are with me, nearer than my breath, closer than my beating heart. You understand my worries better than I do, so let me trust in you and your peace, and calm will overcome my fears.
Amen.

Choose someone to start a "thank you" prayer to Jesus. Then, in turn, offer your own thanks.

MEDIUM ACTIVITY

COLOUR ME IN

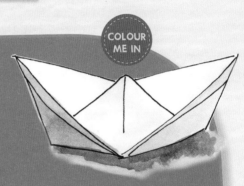

HOW TO MAKE A LIFE JACKET

Imagine you are in the boat with Jesus and the disciples. The storm begins to rage.

First, heavy rain batters the boat.

1 Tear off one end of the boat.

Then the waves break into the boat.

2 Tear off the other end of the boat.

Finally, lightning strikes the mast.

3 Tear off the tip of the sail to form a "U" shape.

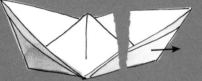

Jesus wakes up and looks at the disciples. He says, "Quiet now, be calm". His words are like a life jacket, helping the disciples to stay afloat; they put their trust in Jesus.

4 Unfold the remains of the boat to see it turn into a life jacket.

BLESSING AND SACRAMENTS

A SIMPLE BLESSING

If you have not made your First Holy Communion, your parish priest (or the priest who visits the hospital) may want to give you a special blessing.

Chaplain/
priest:

The chaplain will begin by saying:
The peace of the Lord be with you always.

Child,
visitor:

And with your spirit.

The chaplain will read a story from the Bible, like the one below.
A reading from the holy Gospel according to Mark.

Glory to you, O Lord.

Mark 10:13-16

People were bringing little children to him for him to touch them. The disciples turned them away, but when Jesus saw this he became angry and said to them, "Let the little children come to me; do not stop them; for it is to such as these that the kingdom of God belongs. I tell you solemnly, anyone who does not welcome the kingdom of God like a little child will never enter it." Then he put his arms round them, laid his hands on them and gave them his blessing.

The Gospel of the Lord.

Praise to you, Lord Jesus Christ.

The priest may then help you to think about the reading and how you think Jesus might be speaking to you today. What would you say to him? Then you might say the Lord's Prayer together.

Before he gives the blessing, the priest will say:
God of love,
ever caring,
ever strong,
stand by us in our time of need.
Watch over your child (name) who is sick,
look after him/her in every danger,
and grant him/her your healing and peace.
We ask this in the name of Jesus the Lord.

 Amen.

The priest will then reach across and make the sign of the cross on your forehead, saying:
 (Name) when you were baptised,
you were marked with the cross of Jesus.
I make this cross ✠ on your forehead
and ask the Lord to bless you,
and restore you to health.

 Amen.

 He will then say:
May the blessing of almighty God,
the Father, and the Son, ✠ and the Holy Spirit,
come upon you and remain with you for ever.

 Amen.

While he is saying these words, you can make the sign of the cross.

RECEIVING THE SACRAMENTS

Jesus wishes to visit us while we are in hospital, much like our family and friends. Jesus visits us in the form of the Simple Blessing and Jesus also visits us through the sacraments. There are three sacraments that you might receive during your stay in hospital.

COLOUR ME IN

1. RECONCILIATION

2. HOLY COMMUNION

3. ANOINTING OF THE SICK

HARD ACTIVITY

Unscramble the letters to make a word:

V E E R G O S S F I N

CLUE : You can find this word somewhere on page 34.

ANSWER: FORGIVENESS

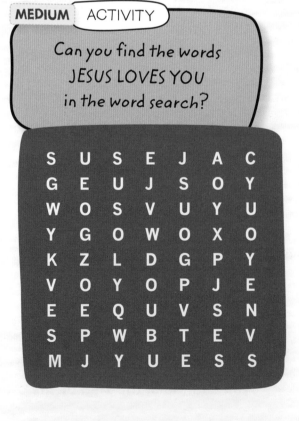

MEDIUM ACTIVITY

Can you find the words JESUS LOVES YOU in the word search?

```
S  U  S  E  J  A  C
G  E  U  J  S  O  Y
W  O  S  V  U  Y  U
Y  G  O  W  O  X  O
K  Z  L  D  G  P  Y
V  O  Y  O  P  J  E
E  E  Q  U  V  S  N
S  P  W  B  T  E  V
M  J  Y  U  E  S  S
```

1. RECONCILIATION:
time to say sorry

If you have been to confession before, you might like to celebrate the sacrament of reconciliation while in hospital. You can ask to see your parish priest (or the priest who visits the hospital).

The priest will begin with the sign of the cross.

In the name of the Father, and of the Son, and of the Holy Spirit.

Amen.

The priest will remind you that God loves you, and ask you what you want to talk about. He may read a short story from one of the Gospels to help you think about how God feels when we hurt other people, and how happy God is when we try to change and become more like Jesus.

Then you can tell the priest about the times when you did not love God or other people. The priest will ask you how you can make things better and suggest a penance – something you can do to make a start. This may be praying for other people in hospital or for your family, and it will help to bring you back to God, by caring for his people.

Complete the prayer to make it your own.

Dear Jesus, things went wrong today and I chose to

....

....

....

....

Help me to remember that you are here guiding and helping me to start again. Thank you. Amen.

Act of Contrition

You can then say this Act of Contrition,
also known as the "sorry prayer":

O my God, I thank you for loving me.
I am sorry for all my sins,
for not loving others and not loving you.
Help me to live like Jesus
and not sin again.
Amen.

The priest will put his hands over your head and
say a special prayer of forgiveness, which finishes
like this:

I absolve you from your sins, in the name of the Father,
and of the Son, ✠ and of the Holy Spirit. Amen.

The priest's words of forgiveness will bring you close
to God and to the people you will meet every day.

2. HOLY COMMUNION: meeting Jesus

If you have made your First Holy Communion, you might wish to
receive Holy Communion while you are in hospital. Sometimes
there is a special Mass for people in the hospital, or you can
also ask the chaplain or one of your visitors if they could
arrange a visit from a priest or someone who can bring Holy
Communion for you, to receive in a special service.

The priest or other minister will begin by saying:
The peace of the Lord be with you always.

And with your spirit.

The Blessed Sacrament will be placed on the table, and everyone
prays quietly for a few moments. You will then be invited to think
about God's love and the times you need his forgiveness.

You can say:
Lord, have mercy.
Christ, have mercy.
Lord, have mercy.

 The priest will say:
May almighty God have mercy on us,
forgive us our sins,
and bring us to everlasting life. Amen.

 A reading from the Bible will follow. It might be this one:
A reading from the holy Gospel according to Mark.

  Glory to you, O Lord.

Mark 14:22-24

As the disciples were eating, Jesus took some bread, and when he had said the blessing he broke it and gave it to them. "Take it," he said, "this is my body." Then he took a cup, and when he had returned thanks he gave it to them, and all drank from it, and he said to them, "This is my blood, the blood of the covenant, which is to be poured out for many."

 The Gospel of the Lord.

  Praise to you, Lord Jesus Christ.

After this, you will be invited to pray:
Our Father, who art in heaven,
hallowed be thy name;
thy kingdom come,
thy will be done
on earth as it is in heaven.
Give us this day our daily bread,
and forgive us our trespasses,
as we forgive those who trespass against us;
and lead us not into temptation,
but deliver us from evil.
Amen.

You will then receive Holy Communion:
Behold the Lamb of God,
behold him who takes away the sins of the world.
Blessed are those called to the supper of the Lamb.

 You will reply:
Lord, I am not worthy
that you should enter under my roof,
but only say the word
and my soul shall be healed.

 You will then be given the Body of Christ,
and you say:
Amen.

Take some time in prayer and ask God to
care for you, your family, the doctors and
nurses, and the other children in the hospital.

> Dear Jesus,
> thank you for being
> with me in Holy
> Communion. Help
> me to find quiet
> times in this busy
> ward, so that I can
> talk to you and
> listen to your voice.
> Amen.

HARD | ACTIVITY

THE GOOD NEWS GAME

1 Fold the corners
of a square sheet
of paper together
to make two
creases. Open
out again to a
square.

2 Fold the four
corners of
the square
into the
centre.

3 Turn over this
smaller square,
and fold in the
four corners a
second time.

4 All four corners are
folded up so that the
points meet in the
middle. Work your
fingers and thumbs into
the pockets of paper in
each of the four corners.

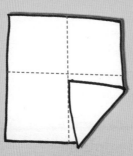

> Play the game and you'll find that everyone is a
> winner when it comes to finding the truth about Jesus!

36

3. ANOINTING OF THE SICK: giving strength

If necessary, your parish priest (or the priest who visits the hospital) may anoint you with the sacrament of anointing.

The sacrament of anointing gives you an opportunity to ask God for extra special help.

When the priest celebrates this sacrament he will anoint you with holy oil.

 The priest will begin by saying:
The peace of the Lord be with you always.

  And with your spirit.

 The priest will then pray, using the following words:
Lord God, you have said to us through your apostle James: "Are there people sick among you? Let them send for the priests of the Church, and let the priests pray over them, anointing them with oil in the name of the Lord. The prayer of faith will save the sick persons, and the Lord will raise them up. If they have committed any sins, their sins will be forgiven them."

Lord, we have gathered here in your name and we ask you to be among us, to watch over our brother/sister (name). We ask this with confidence, for you live and reign for ever and ever.

  Amen.

 Then the priest will lay his hands gently on your head, and he will bless and pray for you.

 The priest will take some oil and anoint you on the forehead, saying:
Through this holy anointing, may the Lord in his love and mercy help you with the grace of the Holy Spirit.

  Amen.

5 Open and close the beak shape until it moves easily forwards and backwards. Mark and colour the Good News game with numbers on the outside and colours on the inside. Under the flaps, write one of the following phrases in each of the segments.

*Pray for someone on the ward.
*Jesus prays with you.
*Jesus listens.
*Jesus loves you.
*Jesus cares for you.
*Help tidy your pillows.
*Jesus is with us for ever.
*Smile and say hello to a nurse.

When we are anointed with oil, we receive a sign of Christ's healing work in action.

Then the priest will anoint you on the hands, saying:
May the Lord who frees you from sin
save you and raise you up. Amen.

After this, the priest will ask you to join him in saying:
Our Father, who art in heaven,
hallowed be thy name;
thy kingdom come,
thy will be done
on earth as it is in heaven.
Give us this day our daily bread,
and forgive us our trespasses,
as we forgive those who trespass against us;
and lead us not into temptation,
but deliver us from evil.
Amen.

The priest will then pray:
Father in heaven,
through this holy anointing
grant (name) comfort in his/her suffering.
When he/she is afraid, give him/her courage,
when afflicted, give him/her patience,
when dejected, afford him/her hope,
and when alone, assure him/her of the support of your holy people.
We ask this through Christ our Lord.

You will answer:
Amen.

The priest will conclude by saying:
May the blessing of almighty God,
the Father, and the Son, ✠ and the Holy Spirit,
come upon you and remain with you for ever. Amen.

Ask your mum or dad to help you make a crown. After you have been anointed, place the crown on your head. You are very special!

Always ask an adult to help you cut out.

Jesus and King David were both anointed with oil. Jesus is King of the Universe and King David was king of Israel (have a look for him in the Bible).

Read the adaptation of 1 Samuel 16:1-13:

The Lord said to the prophet Samuel, "I am sending you to Jesse, who lives in Bethlehem. I have chosen one of his sons to be king. You must anoint him with oil. I will show you which son to anoint." When Samuel saw the first son, he thought, "This must be God's chosen king." He thought this because the first son was tall and handsome. But the Lord said, "No, I don't go by what a person looks like. I go by what is in a person's heart."

When Samuel saw the second son, he thought, "This must be God's chosen king." But again the Lord said no.

Samuel saw the third son, the fourth son, the fifth son, the sixth son, and the seventh son. Each time God said no.

Samuel asked Jesse if he had any other sons. "Yes," said Jesse. "The youngest is looking after the sheep."

They sent for David. When David came, the Lord said, "This is my chosen one. Anoint him." So Samuel anointed David with the horn of oil. The Spirit of the Lord came on David and stayed with him from that day onwards.

David was anointed with oil — a sign of peace. David was a king who brought peace and gladness to the people of God.

PRAYERS TO PICK AND CHOOSE

COLOUR ME IN

If you're feeling unwell, you might like to pray:

I know, Lord, that you have a special love
   for those who are sick.
I am your child; please give me courage,
   heal me, and help me to be happy,
   peaceful and content.
Amen.

A prayer to Our Lady:

Holy Mary,
Mother fair,
filled with love for God,
pray for all our needs.
Pray for us today.

A prayer to say before going to sleep:

God of love, we thank you for today.
We thank you for all its disappointments,
as well as for all its joys.
Forgive whatever we may have done wrong.
We offer you whatever good we have done
today as a share in your work in the world.
Guard and protect us always.
Amen.

This "sorry prayer" might be familiar:

I confess to almighty God
and to you, my brothers and sisters,
that I have greatly sinned,
in my thoughts and in my words,
in what I have done and in what I have failed to do,
(strike your breast for the next two lines)
through my fault, through my fault,
through my most grievous fault;
therefore I ask blessed Mary ever-Virgin,
all the Angels and Saints,
and you, my brothers and sisters,
to pray for me to the Lord our God.

COLOUR
ME IN

A prayer of thanksgiving:

Glory to God in the highest,
and on earth peace to people of
    good will.
We praise you,
we bless you,
we adore you,
we glorify you,
we give you thanks for your great glory,
Lord God, heavenly King,
O God, almighty Father.

Lord Jesus Christ, Only Begotten Son,
Lord God, Lamb of God, Son of the
    Father,
you take away the sins of the world,
    have mercy on us;
you take away the sins of the world,
    receive our prayer;
you are seated at the right hand of
    the Father,
    have mercy on us.

For you alone are the Holy One,
you alone are the Lord,
you alone are the Most High,
Jesus Christ,
with the Holy Spirit,
in the glory of God the Father.
Amen.

Draw, decorate and colour in this page.

FAVOURITE PRAYERS

Draw a picture of yourself here:

My favourite
prayer

My mum's favourite prayer

COLOUR
ME IN

My dad's favourite
prayer

A visitor's favourite prayer

43

PRAYERS FROM THE PSALMS

A prayer for help in times of trouble   Psalm 6:2–4. 8–9

I am worn out, O Lord; have pity on me!
Give me strength; I am completely exhausted
and my whole being is deeply troubled.
How long, O Lord, will you wait to help me?
Come and save me, Lord;
in your mercy rescue me from death.
The Lord hears my weeping;
he listens to my cry for help
and will answer my prayer.

You are my protector   Psalm 43:5

Why am I so sad?
Why am I so troubled?
I will put my hope in God,
and once again I will praise him,
my saviour and my God.

Listen to my prayer, O Lord   Psalm 102:1-2

Listen to my prayer, O Lord,
and hear my cry for help!
When I am in trouble,
don't turn away from me!
Listen to me,
and answer me quickly when I call!

COLOUR
ME IN

A prayer for peace of mind   Psalm 23:1-6

The Lord is my shepherd;
I have everything I need.

He lets me rest in fields of green grass
and leads me to quiet pools of fresh water.

He gives me new strength.
He guides me in the right paths,
as he has promised.

COLOUR
ME IN

Even if I go through the deepest darkness,
I will not be afraid, Lord,
for you are with me.
Your shepherd's rod and staff protect me.

You prepare a banquet for me,
where all my enemies can see me;
you welcome me as an honoured guest
and fill my cup to the brim.

I know that your goodness and love
will be with me all my life;
and your house will be my home
as long as I live.

Wake up, Lord!   Psalm 44:23. 26

Wake up Lord! Why are you asleep?
Rouse yourself! Don't reject us for ever!
Come to our aid!
Because of your constant love, save us!

You may also find the following helpful:

PRAYER OF ST FRANCIS

Lord, make me an instrument of your peace,
Where there is hatred, let me sow love;
Where there is injury, pardon;
Where there is doubt, faith;
Where there is despair, hope;
Where there is darkness, light;
Where there is sadness, joy.

COLOUR ME IN

O Divine Master,
grant that I may not so much seek to be consoled, as to console;
to be understood, as to understand;
to be loved, as to love.
For it is in giving that we receive.
It is in pardoning that we are pardoned,
and it is in dying that we are born to eternal life. Amen.

COLOUR ME IN

GOOD ADVICE

Do not be anxious, the Lord is with you.
Listen to Jesus as he says, "Do not be afraid".
The gentle shepherd loves you and will always
   care for you.
Hear him say, "Peace be with you," and let him
   calm your worries.